DEVASTATING BEAUTY

Poems

by
Gideon Heugh

Copyright © 2018 by Gideon Heugh

All rights reserved

ISBN: 9781976898754

Editor: Megan Rowland

Cover design: Elaine Bentley

*For Emily
and Tabitha*

LIST OF POEMS

Prelude · Dust

DUST 3

I · The Green Lanes

THE GREEN LANES 7
WALKING 8
THE WOODS 10
GARDENING 11
MR ROBIN 12
LINES FOR AUTUMN 13
TO THE UNKNOWN BIRD 14
MOOD MUSIC 15
KINGFISHER 16
MAGPIE 20
SPRING 22
MY GARDEN 23
BLUEBELLS 24
CAMELLIAS 25

II · *Holy Whispers*

CHORUS 29
WAKE UP 30
INK 31
WILLOW 32
RESURRECTION 33
HONEY 34
GOLDFINCH 35
BUTTERFLIES 36
A WINTER'S MORNING IN THE GARDEN.. 37
GULLS 38
HOLY WHISPERS 40
MOMENTS 41

III · *If Only*

WINTER STORM 45
OWL 46
THE BONY NIGHT 47
SPARK 48
IF ONLY 50
ANXIETY ATTACK 52

I'M NOT OLD	53
VOICES	54
MATTHEW 6:25-34	55

IV · Wild Song

PROPHET	59
TURTLE	60
SKY POEM	62
FRUIT	63
LAMENT	64
STALLION	66
WILD SONG	68
I STAND AT THE DOOR AND KNOCK	70
FOX	71
PROGRESS	72
ALBATROSS	73
THE FIGHTBACK	74

Interlude · Beasts

SIP	77
BEASTS	78

SPAGHETTI 80
STATIONERY 82
TO MARY OLIVER 83
THE MOUTH OF A POEM 84

V · What We've Become

LONDON SNOW 87
SNAKES AND LADDERS 88
BIRD BRAINED 89
WHAT WE'VE BECOME 90
JOB DESCRIPTION 92
BINGE 93
WE'VE DONE IT 94
ALL THAT WE HAVE 96
FOUR THOUGHTS ON POSSESSIONS 97
SLUNK 98
CONFINED 99
REST 100
INSTAPOET 102
LOOKING FOR STILLNESS 103
THE WRATH OF GOD 104

VI · *The Great Unbreaking*

BEGINNING 107
STRONGER 108
THE ARRIVAL 110
THE GREAT UNBREAKING 112
DEVASTATING BEAUTY 114

VII · *Rapture*

A PRAYER 119
HUMAN 120
PSALM 126 121
DREAMS 122
HEAVEN 124
SABBATH 125
FREE 126
SLOWLY 127
SAVED 128
BACKFIRE 129
HOLY 130
RAPTURE 132
EXISTENCE 134

CHURCH 135
GOOD NEWS 136

Coda · You

CLEAR BLUE...139
LINES FOR MY UNBORN CHILD 140
YOU 141

Acknowledgments......................................143
About..145

DEVASTATING BEAUTY

Prelude

DUST

'All go to the same place;
all come from dust, and to dust all return.'

– Ecclesiastes 3:20

DUST

We are of the dust,
grounded in dark soil
and the quaking of a new world,
sighed into being by a greater wonder.

We are of the dust,
grainy and awkward
and entirely, astonishingly sacred,
sanctified by a love beyond our wildest dreams.

We are of the dust
yet filled with shimmering glory –
intoxicating holiness not just pouring from heaven,
but rising up through our dirt-covered roots.

Part I

THE GREEN LANES

'The miracle is not to walk on water.
The miracle is to walk on the green earth.'

– Thich Nhat Hanh

THE GREEN LANES

Busyness is prodding me again –
goals and projects and get-up-and-go.

But if I am still,
and I close my eyes,
I hear another call:
the rumble of the distant hills,
the whisper of the wise trees,
the old ways, the green lanes
say, Here.

So I get up, and I go.

WALKING

Solvitur ambulando.

You mustn't be afraid
to laugh in the world's face
and say 'I don't know' –

life is too short
and too important
to be taken seriously –

release your soul
from its consumer cage
and watch it grow

until it fills the air
and colours the world
beautiful.

Learn the small things
and be satisfied:
the rainbow splash of wildflowers,

the swooning moon in crystal night,
the laughter of a chalk stream
as it falls towards a greater sea

. . .

as we all do, maybe.
One foot in front of the other repeated
will often tell you enough,

one foot in front of the other
repeated
will often tell you enough.

THE WOODS

The woods are full of stories.
When we, empty,
pass through them,
all those light-dappled words
seep into us
making us a gift of gold.

When we leave
and go back
to the grey places
the stories leak out
until we are empty
again.

GARDENING

I sit in my well-summered garden
and see beauty
spilling
from every corner:

the pink seduction of the hydrangeas,
the care-free dance
of the lemon-curd butterfly,
the bold silhouette of a bird
joy-riding on a thermal.

The flowers need watering.
As I carefully tip the can
I see that heaven
is a simple thing.

MR ROBIN

What a beautiful song you sing,
Mr Robin.
I love how it opens the sky
leaving room
for a thousand kinds of delight.

Why is it you sing,
Mr Robin?
Did you receive a promotion at work?
Did you clinch the deal?
Did you buy yourself a little something?

What a notion.
I think you sing
because you are alive;
you lack the things to which people cling,
and that is glorious.

LINES FOR AUTUMN

Leaves make their golden turn
unhurried,
then in cooler air
waltz to the damp ground
and in sweet-scented crowd
make happiness
for wellington boots.

TO THE UNKNOWN BIRD

I do not know your name,
wild singer,
or if you are as lovely
to the eyes
as to the ears.

But as winter wraps its pale fingers
around me, around everything,
your voice makes the gloom
irrelevant.

Your flourishes and your trills
and those notes that rhyme with holy
are laying something to rest within me,
yet I do not know your name.

I suppose that not everyone,
if anyone,
knows the true name of God.
I doubt he is diminished by the fact.

Listen to his messengers,
those wild singers.

MOOD MUSIC

I put on some music,
trying to catch a mood,
but the invented rhythms
do nothing.

So I listen instead
to the cackle and spit of the fire,
the roar and hiss of the rain,
the howl and whip of the wind

and ah,
yes,
there it is.

KINGFISHER

1
I long to be delivered
from the ordinary –
but do not think
that by extraordinary
I mean something achieved
or strived for.

You cannot strive for the sky,
all you can hope for
is to dangle beneath its enormous heart
as it circulates the mysteries.

2
I went for a walk today
and it was enough to save my life.

I'd been dying for the usual reasons:
thoughts about money and work
and What Should I Do Next –
those common killers.

Walking is the cure
for the diseases we make.

. . .

3
It's Friday, late January,
the sun and moon in the same sky,
blossoms of creamy cloud
drifting across the blue,
all part of the same dance
that if we paid more attention to
might make words like ambition
seem as ridiculous as they are.

The larger air holds all the answers,
or at least the most important one.

4
I stepped out of my door optimistic,
but was quickly put back
into our world.

The Basingstoke Canal had been drained –
some flooding prevention measure
because, you know, climate change.
There in the pungent sludge
was what you might expect, sadly:
cans, bottles,
plastics and metals
so casually tossed aside

so permanently
sickeningly
there.
I resigned myself
to despair, again.

But then
something seared itself
so hot and bright
into my soul
that all of the ordinary
was burned away.

God's finger
touched
that little corner of Surrey
and I saw the blue spark of static,

a Kingfisher,
unmistakable,
incandescent,
flew
in a bolt
in a flash
in a blink
across our ugliness
and with a flourish
painted life gorgeous.

. . .

It settled upon a winter-bare branch
and sat there, unfiltered.

5
If he who made the bird
made me
then why on earth
would I ever feel the need
to add anything to myself?

I stood
and I stared
smiling
because, what else?

Time ceases to exist
when beauty shows up,
and I only fell from my revelry
when my body remembered the cold.
So I left, reluctantly,
but not without looking over my shoulder
at that royal wonder.

MAGPIE

One for sorrow,
she hops on the crystal frost
while the blue tits pretend not to watch
flitting and twitting
in the sleeping chestnut tree.

She pecks at fallen twigs,
one, two, three,
too small for a proud mother-to-be,
but here's a stick big enough for her,
so she picks it up, looking absurd,
tries to take wing but then flops to earth,

the blue tits tumble over the air
in fits of giggles,
Maggie straightens and ignores their jibes,
she knows she could take them
but doesn't have the time.

She circles the stick,
takes a good look at it,
tries and then fails again,
tries and then fails.

When you know that spring is coming,
when you know there'll be precious eggs

in need of your care
you suck in hope
out of the cold winter air.

She grabs it
and with flaps of primal purpose
beats the whole earth down
launches into the chestnut
barrels and barges
makes her way up the branches
until she reaches the homely bundle
at the top,
of course she'd build it right at the top.

She puts the sticky brick in place,
caws in failure's face,
and then
begins again.

One for sorrow,
but damned if it will be hers.

SPRING

It happened overnight.
One day we were sat inside
shivering against winter's grey grip
when suddenly, wonderfully,
bright fingers of life
surged up from the ground
to pull a new light down,

then all the stillness
and muted colour
was stirred up
into a humming
sun-touched riot –
yellow and purple splashes
and green upon green.

MY GARDEN

It isn't neat
or well thought out.
It won't win any awards.

There are weeds everywhere –
daisies and dandelions
improvising on the lawn.

The lavender is leaking onto the path
and the wildflowers I sowed last year
seem oblivious to order and reason.

What a kick of life though,
what a spill of beauty,
what vibrant droplets of colour
are splashing all around me,

what a mess,
what a gorgeous mess.

BLUEBELLS

We all need music,
our spirits long for it,
and what better melody
than the chiming of the bluebells
ringing out in the woods
like a thousand spring weddings.

CAMELLIAS

It was a dark spring, cold,
with the news hammering home
saying don't hold too close
to the hope that you've known.

But the camellias didn't care.
They staged a coup in the night
and by morning had raised their flags
of bright pink hallelujahs.

Part II

HOLY WHISPERS

'Faith is the bird that feels the light
when the dawn is still dark.'

– Rabindranath Tagore

CHORUS

People ask me why I wake
at the trembling lip of day.

There are a hundred reasons.

But if the only one
was to hear the birds
rhapsody the darkness away,
well that would be enough.

WAKE UP

The wind swims its way
around suburban lanes
singing whale-song to a man
who dreams
of joining it.

Rise! is the cry –
a call to action
diving from the sky –

why moor yourself
to an un-wandering life;
you have been called by the wind
now go: take flight.

INK

I long to rise early and live
the full lightness of morning,

soul making music
with poetry and prose,

thoughts from a higher place
grounded by paper and pen,

I long for dawn's rosy fingers
to be stained with ink.

WILLOW

Mother of pearl sky,
quiet but for pigeon coos
rippling through hopeful stillness.

I can see a willow
from my bedroom window.
It is waiting for something.

Its branches are like lanky ghosts,
the wind tries to set them loose
but the tree, politely stubborn

clings on, knowing that the year
has turned, knowing that soon,
soon, they'll come back to life.

RESURRECTION

Another morning,
another opportunity
to greet the glowing earth with a smile
and say thank you,

another chance to take life by its velvet hand
and step wide-eyed into whatever is now,
another day piled high with moments
like soft play ready to be happied into.

Every morning a miracle, every sunrise
a redemption, a fresh start,
a resurrection. Whatever brokenness
that came before can, little by little,
be repaired by the dawn.

HONEY

Light flows from the sky
slowly, thickly,
like honey
off a spoon,

it drips
onto hungry lips
and we lick
the good morning.

GOLDFINCH

The window
is leaking tree
filling morning
with liquid green
carrying goldfinch
into my skin
I sink
into songlight.

BUTTERFLIES

Two blue butterflies
transfiguring the morning

they must be shavings
of the stained-glass sky

sent here to tell me
to stop wondering why

and just be. Two blue butterflies
trying to set me free.

A WINTER'S MORNING IN THE GARDEN

Frosty, brittle blue dawn;
shed smells like birdseed
and honest work.

A steaming mug of coffee
warms and wakes me
while the starling
delicately breaks her fast
on sunrise-orange berries.

I write
of a smiling earth.

GULLS

It began unremarkable,
rolling to work
trailing fumes
along a tarmac scar.

I do this almost every day
for shame.

The light
had only just got going –
that is, the light that wasn't
some plugged-in neon shriek –

but then everything
became astonishing
all at once

from below the line of trees
there rose
a river of gulls
like some ancient god
surging up
from somewhere deeper
than the world

. . .

so sudden
so shocking
my jaw bowed
as this legion spirit
in a storm
flooded over the motorway.

And just like that they vanished.

And just like that
my day was marked
with lightning
and with life
and with the gulls.

HOLY WHISPERS

Early light splash, blackbird aria
softly revealing colour delight.

Breeze tickles sleepy trees,
those green-strong sentinels

quietly gentling the air
against our carelessness.

Leave anger be.
Let easy horizon stillness lift burdens,

hear the shy, holy whispers
asking us to stop.

MOMENTS

We are undone
and remade

by timid,
fleeting moments.

Don't be so brash
as to scare them away;

don't be in such a hurry
that you miss them.

Part III

IF ONLY

'Therefore do not worry about tomorrow,
for tomorrow will worry about itself.
Each day has enough trouble of its own.'

— Matthew 6:34

WINTER STORM

The lairy wind
with its calloused hands
is sweeping away
clouds of snow
from rooftops

in tantrum
it kicks around
with steel-capped boots
great shouts of powder
from the ground

and grabs hold
gnarly-fingered
the flakes falling down
flinging them
through the air.

Sitting inside, with an orderly pile of work,
I wish that I was out there.

OWL

I know your form, anxiety,
I know your shape,
I know the wounds from which you were born
and the black noise you make.

There is a field, laid out
in the hollow hours of the night,
pressed upon by snow,
silent as a held breath –

suddenly its fabric is impaled
by the screaming owl
surging down
like an apocalypse;

it snatches the small lump of life –
unknowing then all-knowing at once –
and with a whump of its wings
flies home to darkness.

Again the field
dare not breathe.
Let me tell you
what anxiety is like for me.

THE BONY NIGHT

Eyes open, breath short, no sky to speak of.
I wish this was some 'too full of life for sleep' moment,
but I'm not that lucky, or happy.
Stress woke me, anxiety followed through.

I switch on all the lights,
and my environmental conscience
can bite me.
I was always afraid of the dark –

it emaciates reality,
bringing closer some other place
full of the pale half-things
that you would rather forget.

I go outside in my dressing gown,
but the wind and rain
are whispering black revels
into the ears of a thin world

so I go back inside, but not before
I hear one lone singer, braving the bony night.
It's a tentative call,
and so far from dawn,
lonely.

SPARK

5.30am. I'm awake
because of work, but perhaps also
because I'm looking for a spark
in the darkness.

I step outside into heavy-eyed January.
Coffee keeps me safe.

The blackbirds are doing their best,
but already the traffic is shoving them aside;
then, for emphasis, a plane.
How can a little spark survive
the onslaught of progress?

I look up at infinity,
wondering what I might find.
The Plough twinkles down,
so impossibly far that, yes,
I feel something.

Someone has smudged the moon
with a snail trail of cloud,
or maybe smog.

I would slump and go back inside,
but then the plane is gone

and the traffic relents
and there! The blackbirds can hear
one another again. I can hear
their love for an uncommuting life.

I hope there is something within me
for the spark to ignite.

IF ONLY

Last night I fell
into a cold pool of melancholy.

I thought that perhaps when I woke
the mood would have stayed behind,
but it seems to have stalked me
through night's black madness.

If only I weren't shaped by feeling,
if only I didn't bow
to the whims of human,
if only I could align myself
with the movements of heaven
despite the world trying to pull me
in a different direction.

If only I could be holy,
by which I mean knowing
what life truly is.

If only I could bridge
that terrible gap
between who I am
and who I want to be.

. . .

If only it were that easy,
as easy
as falling
into a cold pool.

ANXIETY ATTACK

dropping fast
                lurching
brittle gut
                shaking
darkness
                injecting
rusty mouth
                breaking
hyper nerves
                biting
frightened mind
                fighting
when and why
                losing
paper breath
                leaving
rattled heart
                beating
out of time

I'M NOT OLD

Heavy drops of rain on the roof
sound like old joints popping,
in my head at least.

I'm not old,
or so the statisticians tell me,

but I remember a time
when my knees didn't ache.
I remember a time
when I would look ahead
rather than back.

Now all my joints crack,
like heavy drops of rain
on the roof.

VOICES

There are voices
like earwigs
wriggling in my head,
laying their sharp little eggs,

they hatch
and breed
until my mind
is a writhing mess.

Someone once told me
that I was a failure,
that nothing I ever did
was good enough,

a girl once left me
she told me
that the love I had
wouldn't be enough.

Voices
wriggling
writhing
nibbling.

. . .

But there is another voice,
like the roar
of a storm
in the whisper
of the dawn
that says

you are shining
and exquisite
you are more than enough
and you are exactly
what the world needs.

Which voice I listen to
is up to me.

MATTHEW 6:25-34

I've opened my mind too many times
out of night and into a sinking feeling,
a hollowness into which tumbles
let's say everything.

I hear the first euphoric notes
of the dawn chorus
shine out with such truth
that it makes me ache.

The birds. They don't worry
about what the day might bring,
just a faint tremor of light
is enough to make them praise and sing

and declare goodness over the world.
No resolutions for them, no grand ideas,
no desire to change into something else;
they simply fulfil their beautiful purpose,

which is enough and always will be.
Why do they fly? Not because they have wings.
They have no plans, no ambitions, no things
to weigh them down.

Part IV

WILD SONG

'The idea of wilderness needs no defence,
it only needs defenders.'

– Edward Abbey

PROPHET

I wonder why you brought me
to these splintering days,
this age of earth-death
and default extinction
and the smothering of constellations,

>nostalgia claws at me
>screaming *send me back,*

then I sense a fire that doesn't consume,
a cloud of breath-taking holiness
passing across the face of a mountain
and it says

>I put you here to see,
>to see and hear and feel
>the agony.
>I needed someone whose heart would break,
>who would fall to their knees
>screaming
>*send me.*

TURTLE

My first awareness is struggle,
pushing head
through sleek white egg
to try and make a miracle.

A few minutes
membrane breaking
soft quiet cracks
then free,
first breath,
saltiness of sea.

All is instinct in new life,
I follow the moon home
flippers fast to escape land
leaving tracks on warm sand
until it gets wet,
keep going
until everything is wet.

Yet new eyes are distracted,
bright lights
turn brothers and sisters away
onto tarmac into drains
so freshly alive but then
splat, out go their brains.

Shells aren't quite as hard
as human hearts.

But as for me it's swim swim swim,
soak in the deep profound,
hear the muffled symphony-sound
of water everywhere,

free, oh so free,
until the plastic throttles me.

SKY POEM

I look up
at the blue embrace of sky,
its arms open wide,
trying to hold a world
that's doing its best
to kill it.

FRUIT

There's something in the air again
has the world begun to care again?
No it's just the fumes again
they're making me confused again
body and brain abused again
by cars and planes and factories again
and where exactly are the trees again?
Did we lose the birds and bees again?

Look up with your eyes again
they're smoking out the skies again
telling the same lies again
pretending that we're wise again
when I can hear my children's cries again
daddy what's an elephant again?
Tell them it's not relevant again
we killed them for the hell of it again.

We won't make these mistakes again
the world will never break again
we can't listen to the snake again
when there's no more fruit to take again.

LAMENT

I've never seen starlings
murmerate the sky;
I've never heard the nightingale
cast its magic into the dark;
I'll never compose an ode
to the ascent of the skylark.

The cuckoo doesn't signal
the start of spring for me;
nor does the tree-pipit
sing my summer's shade;
the wren will never give me
a winter serenade.

My garden will never be
a cosy home for hedgehogs;
nor will it ever hum
with the diligence of bees;
there are no butterflies
staccatoing the breeze.

I stand by the edge of the river
but there's nothing there but me,
no salmon are glorying in the jump
no trout are glinting free,

the heron and the otter
are nowhere to be seen.

All of England is empty.
It no longer thrums
to the hum of wild, wild life.
All I feel now is silence,
thanks to our plastic, our chemicals,
our tarmac violence.

STALLION

You of the mustang blood
and the steppe-longing;
you of the easy grace
and the rippling strength
and the mane flowing,
knowing the joy-dancing freedom
of the wild run.

You are led, blinkered,
from one cage
to another
until
BANG
off running
in fear in fear
hot stripe of pain
hot stripe of pain
running
too fast
and fear
hot stripe of pain
and jump
crash
leg snap
hot stripe of pain.

. . .

They put you in another cage
until
BANG
shoot you dead.

Meanwhile the pissed rich
cheer on, leer on, make their money
or lose it, it doesn't matter
you don't matter
all that matters
is the sick thrill of the race.

In my heart, for my comfort,
you are somewhere else now,
mane flowing.

WILD SONG

I take a journey outdoors
looking for a wild song
but when I get there I find
that all the wild's gone

the fields are all empty
the badgers have been shot
the fox has been ripped apart
by the bitch of some toff

the trees are being shredded
the hedgehogs splattered
the bees made extinct
as if they never really mattered

the fish are gone from the sea
but it's stuffed full of plastic
we pretend the end of the world
isn't really that drastic

the hills aren't alive
there is no more music
whatever life we find
we exploit and abuse it

. . .

our waste is piled up
on every tarmac-smothered street
you can't hear the birds singing
but you can read a hundred tweets

on that life-numbing screen
that's made you its slave
by the time you look up
there'll be no more world to save.

I STAND AT THE DOOR AND KNOCK

I stand outside
the barred church doors
hammering with my fists
while around me
the world dies.

I don't want to be let in,
but pray
for those inside
to come out
and join the fight.

FOX

I was a roamer,
a field tripper,
a rangy loper,
a brush with something
deeper than suburban.

See just a glimpse of me,
always just a glimpse –
primal eyes
and coat like wildfire,
tail dipped in mountain-peak.

Curled together
I cleaned my scrubby cubs
with a rough tongue,

look at it now,
draped on the tarmac,
my body a dirty pink smear,

not even given
the blessing of the soil.

PROGRESS

The voices from the wilderness
– so necessary, so healing –
are being drowned out
by the violent bell
of progress.

The mass-produced madness
of rabid consumerism
has pinned nature
to a cold concrete floor,
one hand around her neck,
the other hungrily searching
for whatever it can get.

And the voices
from the wilderness
whisper
please stop.

ALBATROSS

Sea mapper,
cloud knower,
great winged ranger
crossing continents of air,
sailor's charm,
poet's muse.

You see something
that looks like fish,
scoop it up
then take it back
for the hungry little mouths,

how are you to know
that you're filling your babies with plastic

how are you to know
why they suddenly lie dead

how are you to know
that we've given up shooting you
and are doing this instead.

THE FIGHTBACK

I see the thinning of the earth,
I feel it in my marrow,
in my shuddering gut.

My heart leaks a ragged lament,
unable to look away
from the fault lines we've made

in this ball of water and dirt,
this miracle home
of devastating beauty.

Something grows from my depths,
whispering above the despair
how do we fight back?

I look at my shaking hands,
my rusted coil of feelings,
and, after a time, decide.

Interlude

BEASTS

'To pay attention, this is our endless and proper work.'
— Mary Oliver

SIP

Words. Words are like
a warm mug of coffee
(or tea if you insist)
into which I've stirred
the honey
of flower-hopping bees
and the rich milk
of grass-happy cows.

I hold it firmly in my hands,
its scent a prayer
for the sacred early hours.

Sip on the words,
let their heat slowly fill you,
let their light uncover buried things,
let their texture smooth out
the roughness of worry.

BEASTS

Poems can seem a bit silly,
can't they?

People splaying open
their feelings
and observations
and grandiose opinions

in a way that says
aren't I clever?

I can't pretend this is anything different.

We are beasts of language,
all of us,
whether we like it or not.

Mostly we talk
or these days
tap with our thumbs
and we're polite
and that's fine.

But sometimes you need to snarl,
sometimes you need to howl,
sometimes you need to sing out your soul

for the bird in the other tree
or weep

in a way that says
isn't the beauty of the world
astonishing?

And these
wild noises
are poems.

SPAGHETTI

The Professors and the Critics say
that if we self-publish
we will never become one of them.
What a shame.

I guess we'll leave them
to gush-splutter their praise
upon whatever the Glittering Literary World
has thrown up recently,

then we'll hunt down words
that hollow us out with scalpels
and fill us spoonful by spoonful
with golden dirt
or carefully angled starlight
or the crushing expanse of the cola-dark sea,

we'll seek out those primal hallelujahs
and angsty incantations
thrown at our walls like spaghetti,
hoping to stick, perhaps to stain,

we'll pray with late-night journal scribbles
and teenage heart-ache psalms bleeding
and bleeding and we'll mop it up hoping
it can be anything other than red.

. . .

Not every poem has to be a thunder-muttering sonnet
or a scandi-sparse postmodern bullshit;
if a poet falls over in a wood
and makes a snow-angel in the pine-needles
it doesn't matter if the only ones to hear his laughter
are the nuts, and the trees.

STATIONERY

Too many words have leaked from me
without finding anything to soak them up.
They spill from my spirit, drip from my skin,
but where do they go without paper and pen?
Perhaps some other writer will find them,
pick them up and use them
in a way that I have failed to do.
Oh that we wouldn't be so wasteful,
that no word would be lost
to unforgiving nylon carpets
or gum and spit-sprayed pavements.
Like these words – these words, which I'll never lose.
Keep your stationery close, mop up any spill,
For words have a purpose, a destiny to fulfil.

TO MARY OLIVER

Thank you for teaching me
that poetry
needn't be
pretentious
or impenetrable.

Thank you for teaching me
that poetry
can simply be
the tremor of a sob,
or the running of a stream
over rock,
or the sound that morning makes
when no one else is awake.

THE MOUTH OF A POEM

The mouth of a poem might be a rip,
a slit, a thin acre of glass
passing through the heart;
it might be the uncurling of a leaf
or a puncture of belief
or drawing back the curtains
to watch the trees stir up daylight.
It could be water slumping
around your dipped finger,
or a star collapsing
somewhere unreachable
but present through the violent feel of it all;
many things might lick the back of a word
and stick it to a hopeful, crumpled envelope.

Part V

WHAT WE'VE BECOME

'You can best serve civilization by being against what usually passes for it.'

— Wendell Berry

LONDON SNOW

The snow never settles
on Oxford Street,
there is no blanket
to hush it to sleep,

too many cars,
too many feet
in a hurry to be
wherever,

their hands full
of the bustle and clatter,
no time to look
at the things that matter,

no time to reach down
cup the divine
then throw it
at someone else.

SNAKES AND LADDERS

people
who
spend
their
lives
climbing
the
ladder
of
success
will
reach
the
top
and
realise
there's nothing there

BIRD BRAINED

The cuckoo,
whom I can hear
blessing the spring
over a rugged dale
in Cumbria
arrived
from beyond the Sahara
navigating
by God only knows what.

And we need Google Maps
to get to the shops.

WHAT WE'VE BECOME

We no longer make:
hands that should caress and work and shape
now do nothing
but hold the things we've bought
and then a little later
throw them away.

We no longer do:
our wild-strong bodies that should be
dancing and running and loving
are sat still, muscles wasting, backs aching
not from a day in the fields hay-making
but from watching it on a pastoral period drama.

We no longer see:
our miracle eyes that can take in
the vastness of skies
or find the singularity of another soul
are locked numbly onto screens,
looking for five reasons to exist.

We no longer hear:
there's too much noise drowning out
the still small voice of calm
and we don't know the names of the birds

that fling their souls upon the gloom
even as we make them extinct.

We no longer are:
the delicate glory of our being
has been diluted by digital
smothered by concrete and plastic and steel
and all our morbid creations,
which will never be as alive as we once were.

JOB DESCRIPTION

Are you ambitious?
Do you want to work in a fast-paced environment?
Do you want to succeed whatever it takes?

Not really,
but I do want to vomit.

I look from the glare of the computer
to the gentler light of the window,
see the trees on the other side.

They sway, perhaps a motion of pity,
then quietly, slowly,
continue the tender business
of being themselves.

BINGE

We have a shiveringly brief amount of time
to soak in the awe and wonder
of this glimmering world

but here: spend hour after hour
after hour
of your unrepeatable days
sat still in front of a screen,
outsourcing your life

to YouTube
and Netflix
who get rich
off our flabby
flaccid
apathy.

WE'VE DONE IT

The small things can hurt the most,
though I'm not saying 50 elephants
killed every day
for the ivory trade
doesn't pierce me.

Anyone who has lived long enough
has felt the earth thinning.
Perhaps one year the cuckoo
stopped coming back.
Perhaps the bees
that used to flood your lavender
no longer show up.
In summer, how many species
of butterfly did you see?
I counted just three.

We've unmade the world.

Yet it wasn't through murderous rage,
no violent desire to extinguish
our mother's vibrant lights.
No, it wasn't that.

. . .

But we do want supermarket aisles
stuffed with all the choices,
we want every kind of meat
we want all you can eat
we want next day delivery
with all the latest tech and trends

yes: we are why the world ends.

ALL THAT WE HAVE

Our phones are diminishing us,
providing glossy pleasures
instead of rich, deep, earthy ones;
leading us away from here and now
to somewhere less human, less wild,
less connected to the people all around,
less receptive to the sights and sounds of life –
full, audacious, love-spilling life,
which we've swapped for a rectangle of anxiety.

Nothing you find online could ever replace
looking into someone's eyes;
nothing digital could ever compete
with the touch of a hand, the warmth of an embrace.
We are all that we have,
we were made for each other,
so why not switch it off
and simply be with one another.

FOUR THOUGHTS ON POSSESSIONS

1
Possessions:
dark, heavy anchors
tying us to a life
that is less.

2
The more stuff
you pour into your life
the more dilute
you become.

3
We buy to try and fill
an emptiness
into which will only fit
things that are free.

4
'Rabbi, what is the key
to eternity?'
'Give everything away,
laugh, dance, and follow me.'

SLUNK

The damp, lonesome wind
tap taps at the door,
wanting to come in.

A voice inside says
No! we're happy slunk
in our slouching
and our gorging
and the glare of the TV
is fuzzing
in our eyes.

Still the lonesome wind knocks,
wanting to come in.

CONFINED

I'm lost indoors,
drained of my fleshy might,
nothing to stir my inner light.

I'm hopeless indoors,
trapped, fractured, at my worst,
nothing to quench that green-fingered thirst

for wild things. I'm surrounded by walls
and ticking clocks and humming machines,
nothing to fire my bones, my sap, my dreams.

REST

We've become
all of us
citizens of screenland,
switching on something
to try and switch off,
encouraged to escape
our thunderous minds;
numbing feeling, dumbing sense,

is that really rest?

You are far more interesting
than the world would have you believe,
and you shouldn't be afraid
to spend time with yourself
with nothing but yourself

in the silences,
in the gaps.

What you will find
is that within you
are thirsty roots
and resurrections
and a pulsating, luminous hope.

. . .

True rest doesn't mean tuning out,
it means tuning in
to you;

true rest means coming alive to our senses
and leaning over to look
at the dark pool of our feelings;

true rest means giving space
for the soul to sing
or sob
or whatever it needs,

it means opening up
so there's room
for a new thing
to sink in.

INSTAPOET

You deserve better than instapoetry.
You deserve better than thin lines
serving up vague truths
and fortune-cookie platitudes,
you deserve better than hollow words
thumbed onto pretty pixels
in the name of a shallow double-tap
before your tired eyes scroll on.

Poetry should consume,
not be consumed;
it should be wrestled with
like some god in the night
who by morning
might have broken your bones.
You deserve more.
You deserve canticles spat out
by a funeral of nightingales,
you deserve arias carved into your gut
by a banshee or a nymph,
you deserve heart-splinters
squeezed through a tube of lightning
until they bleed hot and spluttering
from the vein of a pen nib.

You deserve poetry.

LOOKING FOR STILLNESS

It's hard to be still
these days.
The world wants us to buzz –
but not like the bee,
who is only looking for colour
and sweet things,
more like the droning of a phone
'Me! Me!'

I'd rather be still,
forget myself,
watch the bee.

THE WRATH OF GOD

Many people are put off
when they think of the wrath of God;
it's hard to reconcile love and rage.

I have some thoughts. They begin
with the black heart of men:
the child abusers,
the traffickers,
the money-hoarders.

I think of how we slaughter the world
so that a few of us can get fat
while the rest starve.
I think of mankind's easy cruelty
and selfish violence
and I take great comfort
in God's vengeance.

Then I look at my own heart,
and thank God for his forgiveness.

Part VI

THE GREAT UNBREAKING

'Behold, I am doing a new thing;
now it springs forth, do you not perceive it?'

– Isaiah 43:19

BEGINNING

Do you see it?
That ember glow on the horizon,
the flicker of courage rising,
the quaking shadows
of dry bones being invited to live.

Do you feel it?
The fierce wave of hearts burning,
the multitude of souls yearning,
begging for a wildfire of grace
to spread across a desperate world.

Do you hear it?
The roar of the broken-hearted,
the rumble of a movement started,
the thunder of justice and love and light –
a cavalry charge of hope in the night.

STRONGER

We're all searching for something true,
surrounded by fake news, extreme views,
everyone's confused
but I've seen that love is stronger than fear,
haven't you?

Sometimes it feels like there's nothing we can do,
we don't know who to trust,
systems are being abused –
it can be lonely when you're searching
for something true.

We're longing for hope,
we're longing for something new,
we're longing for that bitter mountain to be moved;
but I've seen that love is stronger than despair,
haven't you?

Society seems to be in crisis
and perhaps our hearts are too;
but there's a different perspective that you can choose
when you're searching
for something true:

. . .

If you peer behind a veil
that's been torn in two
you'll see the promise of a world renewed –
I've seen that love is stronger than hate,
haven't you?

Maybe that's not enough, maybe we need another clue,
maybe there are some things that will never be proved.
Yet we're all searching for something true,
and I've seen that love is stronger than death,
haven't you?

THE ARRIVAL

With the roar of the throne room still rattling my being
I thunder into the cosmos.

The glory of that higher plane burns hot within me
as I streak past nebulae and galaxies faster than light
and with stars in my wake I hear the singing,
as the hammering together and tearing apart of atoms
violently declares the wonder of the one who sent me.

But my purpose leaves no time for me to pause
and soak it all in,
so I fly and I fly until I feel it approaching –
the Milky Way,
a bright storm of beauty pulsating with expectation.

I am still millions of light years away
but I sense the coming arrival,
so with joy and resolve burning within me
I move towards my goal.

I see the sun, unremarkable in an ocean of stars
yet selected for something greater,
and with solar winds battering against me
I approach the Earth, a delicate blue dot
with life ringing from it like a chorus of bells –

the former seat of Eden,
where a new thing is being done.

Flames roar around me
and a sonic boom shakes the air
as I enter the atmosphere,
homing in on a beacon of hope
that is calling throughout the entire universe.

I land in a hot, dusty village, a nowhere,
and, taking a deep breath, I walk into the house,
holiness shimmering off me like desert heat.
She is there, young as a flower,
kneading dough for their daily bread.

I greet her and tell her she is highly favoured,
that heaven is with her,
then seeing the look in her eyes
I tell her there's no need to be afraid,
I tell her that the miracle of history
will happen through her,
that she has been chosen to give birth to love itself.

Then, my mission complete, I leave.
I fly back home to glory,
trembling in awe and hope.

THE GREAT UNBREAKING

I remember the beginning:
the awe of newness
the sudden weight of time
and the mouth of God
spitting out violent light;

I remember the garden singing with life,
the scent of flowers carried on unpolluted breeze,
tentative footsteps
on never-trodden grass,
man, woman, the first embrace.

I remember the slither of the serpent
and the hiss of the oldest lie;
I remember pain, howling pain
and then the bitterness of shame,
hiding from the only love that could fix it.

I remember the breaking,
relationships ripped apart,
great chasms between people and God
and people and the world
and people and themselves.

. . .

But I also remember him,
the carpenter's son, the Rabbi, the temple-trasher,
demon-tormentor, crowd-feeder, leper-healer;
I remember his body being wrecked –
his brokenness our great unbreaking.

DEVASTATING BEAUTY

On Friday my hope died.
The sky wept itself dark
the ground broke apart
and all creation cried
for the bloodied innocence
hammered into a tree.

There were whispers
of a torn curtain
but they didn't reach my ears
or mend my mangled heart
or stem the bitter tears
as we took
the body
down.

On Saturday we grieved,
hiding from the troops
whom we'd once believed
would be overthrown
by the carpenter's boy,
who had preached
and fed and healed
and was now dead.

. . .

But then on Sunday –
the devastating beauty
of that Sunday –
when time and space
were blown out of shape
and angels wrapped in electric grace
rolled the impossible away,

he is not here
they proclaimed
for glory had risen
our failings were forgiven
and the rules of life and death
were rewritten
as an empty tomb declared:
Love is alive.

Part VII

RAPTURE

'So I will build my altar in the fields,
And the blue sky my fetted dome shall be.'
— Samuel Taylor Coleridge

A PRAYER

Let the air be thick
with the spirit of green, slow things;
let their careful dream-light fill me,
pushing out what the world has put there.

HUMAN

I am not technology.
I am made from mud
and stardust
and the hot breath of God.

I am not smooth or clean.
I scratch and I break
and there is dirt
under my rough fingernails.

I am not machine –
I am creature.
I dance and weep and sweat
and I love with my awkward body.

I am not perfect.
I make people cry
and I fail
and I fall again and again.

I am human.
A messy, heaving,
broken, coarse, yet
somehow glorious, human.

PSALM 126

When we break
it's like
the ploughing of the fields
into which
some higher thing
scatters seeds
too small
to be significant
surely?

We water them
with our tears
and then
forget.

But in the harvest,
my God,
the abundance…

DREAMS

What are your dreams?
Perhaps you've forgotten.

Perhaps you tried to guide them
into the light of day,
but when others saw them
they laughed and scolded
and said, 'That dream does not belong
in the world of teeth and claws
and Settle For Less.'

Hope is a fragile thing
and can break
even in the most careful hands.

So maybe you buried your dreams,
somewhere dark, somewhere deep,
and empty-hearted
you wander the wistful halls
of regret.

However.

There is always a however,
a conjunction connecting us
to the winds of heaven

that since before time
have sought you out,
ready to blow away the heavy dirt
that a heavy world
shovelled on your dreams.

Hope is a stubborn thing
and like an ember
has a wild temper within.

What are your dreams?
Someone hasn't forgotten.
Someone wants to show them
the light of day
and say, *Yes.*

HEAVEN

Beauty
is as essential
to our souls
as water
to our bodies.

A happy life
is quiet simplicity,
selfless sacrifice
and relentless
love.

Seek God
in all things,
sink deep
into the wonder
of creation.

Reach up
and pull heaven down,
fill your cup
then splash it
around.

SABBATH

Clear air sweeps cluttered mind,
leaving space for sacred things
and the largeness of hopeful thought.

Sunday clarity, Sunday catharsis,
caked on weariness crumbles away,
uncovers something radiant.

FREE

You can't earn holiness,
it shies away from striving;
holiness was planted in you
before that first cell divided;
the sacred is in all of us
but some have been forced to hide it
by culture, by religion,
by busyness or by rejection
but it's there: a seed
ready to spring into life.
Holiness is free, as free
as the warmth of the sun
or the refreshment of rain
or another heartbeat, again.

SLOWLY

I go on long walks, read long books.
I cook food slowly and savour,
not caring about convenience, only flavour.
I am here, now, slowly.

I daydream, get lost in my thoughts,
wash the dishes slowly, feeling the suds
slide on the crockery. I make love to my wife
slowly, feel her quiver beneath me.

I touch slowly, breathe in texture, the rough bark
of an old tree, the soothing smoothness of skin,
the slow scratch of this ballpoint pen against
the yellowy-white paper.

I smell rich, deep scents –
the slow euphoria of roses, the cool clarity of dawn,
the possibilities of a new book
or the sun's warm breath on the grass.

I live. I swim
slowly into life,
into all of its wet
shimmering
fullness.

SAVED

The world wants to enter
the temple of my mind
but I tell it

another has been there
giving sight to the blind
and throwing out the money-men

and setting the wild things free.
The world can be unkind,
but the sacred has saved me.

BACKFIRE

You can tell the devil
that the weapons he sent against me
have been stolen
and are in the possession
of someone
with a stronger arm
and a steadier aim
and greater aggression
someone
who is on my side.

HOLY

1
I would like to reclaim the word holy, please.

See, you've made it something
it never should have been,
with your dogma,
your pompous piety,
your boring sermons
and everyone else is the laity.

There are few things more unholy
than 'I am better than you.'

I'm as guilty as anyone.

2
Holy is the smile of a single mother
cradling her newborn baby.

Holy is two people wildly in love
making wild love.

Holy is standing beside a deathbed,
holding a trembling hand.

. . .

3
Whenever we make holy
about rules
and rewards
we give permission
to the hate preachers
and the excluders
and the suicide bombers.

There's nothing holy
about closed hearts
and narrow thoughts.
Holy is as open as the spring;
it as wide as the cosmos
and will fit in the palm of your hand.

Holy is with all of us,
in all of us,
for all of us.

RAPTURE

Have you noticed
that an awful lot of people
spend their lives
trying to get somewhere else?

Normally a place with more
   1) money
   2) time
   3) approval

You can make a lot more of 2
if you stop caring about 1 and 3
and you will often find
exactly where you need to be
when you stop trying to get there.

One of the saddest
and most dangerous things
is people who obsess
over getting to heaven.
I wonder why they do this,
when so much heaven is here.

Perhaps they've never been swallowed by the velvet rose,
or stumbled upon an astonishment of bluebells,
or stood in an English field

while the dawn chorus washes away the stains.
How limp the cynical life must be,
how impotent the life
that doesn't surrender to mystery,
how lost the life that doesn't pause in woodland
to hear and see and breathe
the holiness all around.

Heaven is here,
if you'd only look.

I think that if God wants us to be somewhere
after our time here (and let's stop trying
to answer that question)
then we'll be there,
and our efforts will most likely just muddle things.

There is heaven within you,
in the miracle that is your heart,
in the capacity you have
to hold someone's hand
feel the lightning of their soul
and say, 'I love you,'
or perhaps better yet, 'I forgive you.'

Where is heaven
if it isn't there?

EXISTENCE

If music is nothing more
than vibrations in the air
then why does it create
a world of magic in our minds?

If rainbows are nothing more
than the refraction of photons
then why the wide-eyed delight
whenever one appears?

If the stars are nothing more
than balls of burning gas
they why do they make us stop
and stare, lost in wonder?

If the dawn is nothing more
than the turning of the earth
then how does it make us feel
like heaven is in our heart?

If I am nothing more
than a bag of chemicals and water
then how am I capable of love,
not just a thousand lesser things?

CHURCH

You cannot build God a house.
He has no more preference
for four walls and a steeple
than he does for a copse
or a mountain top
or the lavender in my garden.

The earth is God's house;
He can plant his ladder
anywhere
at any time
for the angels
to flit up and down
like fireflies.

You think we are the only ones to worship God?
What about the jubilation of whales
or the ecstasy of butterflies
or the unyielding praise of the rocks?

You can see the flames of Pentecost every day
as the darkness collapses
around the rising sun,
you can wake up wherever you are and say
surely something capable of hurling stars was here,
shaking me in my sleep.

GOOD NEWS

It's Saturday morning
and I'm as awake as the spring grass.
I consider turning on the TV,
that dark glass of bad news
that we don't really need.

Then out of the corner of my eye
I see a robin
doing the cha-cha
on the bird table,
as if it were a grand ballroom
with the perky flowers
and warm-hearted trees
his appreciative audience.

So I put down the remote,
pull up a chair,
I stop, I stare, and I see
that beneath the sacred blue sky
there is good news.

Coda

YOU

'I wish I could show you
when you are lonely or in darkness,
The Astonishing Light
of your own Being!'

– Hafez

CLEAR BLUE

I never imagined
that I could fly like the birds
until I learned about you.

I never believed
I'd ever feel as free
as the lark on the summer breeze,
or the albatross cruising a thousand skies,
or the cranes flying so high
they make a mockery of mountains.

I thought I'd always be stuck on the ground,
flinging out dreams that would never be found
by whatever it is that makes them come true,

but then I found out about you.

LINES FOR MY
UNBORN CHILD

The world will try to tell you
that you aren't enough,
that you need
that job, that car, those clothes,
that house, that man, that woman
that whatever.

The world will try to tell you
more, you need more.

But something else –
subtle, gentle, yet infinitely powerful
will whisper
you are enough,
precisely and completely
and wonderfully enough.

Your identity was woven in the womb,
perfect before your first breath;
you have the shimmer of the miraculous about you,
the fire of something holy within you;
the wonder of life, always the wonder and beauty of life.

You don't need to do or have
in order to be, because you are.

YOU

You are a wild and gleeful thing,
nudged by lavish grace
towards all the astonishments,
and nothing can stop it
or you.

You are not a mistake.
The earth aches for your singular life,
for the miracle radiance
of purely, specifically
you.

The shakings and the dark noises
of a man-made world
cannot compete with your hallelujah blood,
your hosanna spirit,
or with the gentle fury of hope.

ACKNOWLEDGEMENTS

When I decided to go down the route of self-publishing, I had great visions of striding out confidently alone. I soon realised how ridiculous that was. And so, I owe a great debt to a number of amazing people, without whom this book wouldn't have been possible:

My wonderful editor Megan – thank you for being my Coleridge. The incredibly gifted Elaine – you lifted me up when the weight of this project was pulling me down. Joel – your talent and tenacity have inspired me more than you know. My parents – you have both been sources of much-needed encouragement, love and support. My beautiful wife, Emily – you are everything. And finally, to you, for buying and reading my book – thank you!

ABOUT

Gideon Heugh is a poet, copywriter, environmentalist, gardener, fell walker, bird watcher, runner and coffee drinker. He has a Masters in Creative Writing and works for a humanitarian relief and development agency. He lives in Surrey, England, with his wife and daughter-to-be. *Devastating Beauty* is his first book.

Printed in Great Britain
by Amazon